The Peacemaking Church

Small Group Study

www.hendrickson.com
www.Peacemaker.net

PEACEMAKER®
MINISTRIES

Copyright © Peacemaker Ministries
www.Peacemaker.net
https://pm.training/
Edition 2.1

Published by Hendrickson Publishers
an imprint of Hendrickson Publishing Group
Hendrickson Publishers, LLC
P. O. Box 3473
Peabody, Massachusetts 01961-3473
www.hendricksonpublishinggroup.com

ISBN 978-1-68307-107-5

All rights reserved. No part of this publication may be reproduced, stored in a retrieval system, or transmitted in any form or by any means, electronic, mechanical, photocopying, recording, or otherwise, without prior written permission of Peacemaker Ministries, except by a reviewer who may quote brief passages in a review.

Scripture quotations are taken from the Holy Bible, New International Version. Copyright © 1973, 1978, and 1984 by International Bible Society. Used by permission of Zondervan Bible Publishing House. All rights reserved.

Printed in the United States of America

Third printing Hendrickson Publishers Edition — August 2021

Contents

A Personal Note from Ken Sande 4
As You Get Started 5

Part One: Glorify God
Session 1: Conflict Provides Opportunities 7
Session 2: Live at Peace 11

Part Two: Get the Log Out of Your Eye
Session 3: Conflict Starts in the Heart 15
Session 4: Confession Brings Freedom 19

Part Three: Gently Restore
Session 5: Just Between the Two of You 23
Session 6: Take One or Two Others Along 27

Part Four: Go and Be Reconciled
Session 7: Forgive as God Forgave You 31
Session 8: Overcome Evil with Good 35

Next Steps: Growing and Serving as a Peacemaker 39

Optional Small Group Study Sessions
Optional Session A: Trust in the Lord and Do Good 45
Optional Session B: Is This Really Worth Fighting Over? .. 51
Optional Session C: Speak the Truth in Love 55
Optional Session D: Look Also to the Interests of Others .. 59

Slippery Slope Responses to Conflicts in the Bible 63
Answer Key for Blanks 64

A Personal Note from Ken Sande

God loves to humble and refine me by giving me "homework"!

Today, as I was putting the finishing touches on this study guide, he gave me an opportunity to practice and experience what I teach.

Three months ago, one of our children had a conflict with another child at church. As is so often the case, the kids promptly apologized and moved on, but we parents struggled to lay matters to rest. (Another example of why we should become like children!)

We had a couple of seemingly positive personal meetings, but something still wasn't right. An invisible wall was blocking our friendship. So we turned to our church for assistance, asking a respected Sunday school teacher to help us uncover our blind spots and truly be reconciled.

When the four of us met with him, he helped us to practice all the principles covered in this study. Reminding us how God has forgiven all our sins through the gospel of Christ, he urged us to stop pretending, defending, blaming, and covering up. He helped us to see how pride, bitterness and insensitivity were keeping us apart. He encouraged us to listen carefully and confess thoroughly. Best of all, he rejoiced with us as we finally experienced genuine forgiveness and reconciliation.

As my wife and I drove home, we thanked God that we belong to a church that repeatedly teaches and promotes biblical peacemaking. We also thanked him for giving us gifted leaders who are equipped to help us when we can't resolve conflicts on our own – even when they involve issues that are far more complicated than what we faced this morning.

We pray that God will use this group study to build a similar capacity for peacemaking in your church. As you and others learn what the Bible teaches about peacemaking, you can respond confidently to the conflicts you encounter in your family, church, and workplace. And as you develop your God-given gifts for peacemaking, he may be pleased to use you to help others experience the joy of true reconciliation.

May God use your lifestyle of reconciliation, your family's peace and your church's increasing unity to draw many people to the Prince of Peace, our Lord Jesus Christ.

As You Get Started

Group Setting
This study is designed for *interactive small groups* that meet weekly to study, discuss, pray, and grow together. It can easily be adapted for use in Sunday school classes or evening church services, or by a married couple, or by any group of people who want to grow together as peacemakers.

How Long?
This study is designed to last eight weeks, but for those groups that are so inclined, there are also four optional lessons included in the study materials. (Note: The twelve-lesson format closely follows the twelve chapters in *The Peacemaker*.*)

Context
This study is intended to be one part of a broader initiative toward building a culture of peace in your church. *The Peacemaking Church Resource Set* includes three key components:

- **Inspiring** – Your pastor will preach a sermon series on biblical peacemaking and cast a vision for what a culture of peace looks like in your church.
- **Teaching** – Your entire church will learn the basic principles of personal peacemaking by going through this Small Group Study together.
- **Embedding** – Passionate peacemakers will establish a Peacemaking Team to make peacemaking an ongoing and vital part of your church's life.

If your church is not currently doing all three parts of this initiative, please consider promoting it to your leaders so that your entire church will experience the benefits of biblical peacemaking.

Session Format
Each group session is divided into five sections:

- **Icebreaker** is designed to help your group relax, get to know one another and share what God has been doing in your lives.
- **Learning Together** involves a 25-minute video presentation in which Ken Sande teaches the core principles of biblical peacemaking.
- **What Do You Think?** provides an opportunity to discuss challenging peacemaking concepts and explore ways to apply them in real life.
- **Pray for One Another** allows members of your group to share and pray for one another regarding specific habits they want to change or relationships they are working to reconcile.

The Peacemaker: A Biblical Guide to Resolving Personal Conflict, Ken Sande (Baker Books, 3rd Ed. 2004).

- **My Next Step** provides a practical homework assignment designed to help you apply what you have learned.

Reading and Preparation
- While optional, you will receive the greatest benefit from this study by completing the suggested readings in The Peacemaker each week. For your convenience, this guide offers daily readings of 4–5 pages each.
- Another way to enhance your study is to memorize the Memory Verse and Key Principle given for each session. By hiding these words in your heart and meditating on them repeatedly, you will be prepared to draw on them for prompt and reliable guidance when conflict strikes.
- If you are unable to complete the reading or memory work every week, please participate in the meetings anyway! All of the key concepts will be presented in the teaching video, so you will still be able to participate comfortably and fully in the group discussion.
- Finally, after each session, take the time to complete the suggested My Next Step, then share your experience with the others in your group. God often works most powerfully as you reflect on and seek to apply the principles you learn during each session.

Group Commitment
To enhance the openness and effectiveness of your group, it is helpful for each member to affirm the following values.
- Preparation: I will strive to prepare for each meeting by reading the selected pages and completing each week's My Next Step exercise.
- Attendance: I will strive to attend every meeting, unless illness or unavoidable obligations intervene, and I will call if I expect to be late or absent.
- Breathe grace: I will refrain from criticizing or judging others in thought or word, and I will strive to spur others on in their walk with Christ through gracious, constructive, and encouraging words.
- Iron sharpening iron: Realizing that spiritual growth often requires loving correction, I will humbly receive and consider other's insights on how I can put off worldly ways and grow to be more like Christ.
- Confidentiality: I will carefully guard the trust and confidences of others. I will not discuss outside this group any personal information revealed within the group.
- Newcomers: I will check with our group leader before inviting others to join the group, and I will warmly welcome newcomers.
- Prayer: I will pray regularly for the people in my group.

Session One
Conflict Provides Opportunities

MEMORY VERSE
So whether you eat or drink or whatever you do, do it all for the glory of God (1 Cor. 10:31).

KEY PRINCIPLE
Conflict is an opportunity.

Suggested Weekly Reading in *The Peacemaker*
- Day 1 – Pages 11–16
- Day 2 – Pages 17–22
- Day 3 – Pages 22–29
- Day 4 – Pages 29–34
- Day 5 – Pages 34–41

THOUGHTS AND QUESTIONS
Thoughts or questions that come to my mind as I read, which I can share with my group:

___
___
___
___
___
___
___
___
___
___
___
___
___

Part 1 – Glorify God
How can I please and honor God in this situation?

Group Study

Icebreaker

Learning Together (Video)

1. What is conflict?

   - A _____* in opinion or purpose that frustrates someone's goals or desires. (*Answers for blanks are on page 64.)

2. The Four G's: A God-centered response to conflict
   So whether you eat or drink or whatever you do, do it all for the glory of God. Do not cause anyone to stumble, whether Jews, Greeks, or the church of God—even as I try to please everybody in every way. For I am not seeking my own good but the good of many, so that they may be saved. Follow my example, as I follow the example of Christ (1 Cor. 10:31–11:1).

   - G_____ God (1 Cor. 10:31).
     How can I please and honor God in this situation?

   - G_____ the log out of your eye (Matt 7:5).
     How can I show Jesus' work in me by taking responsibility for my contribution to this conflict?

   - G_____ restore (Gal. 6:1).
     How can I lovingly serve others by helping them take responsibility for their contribution to this conflict?

   - G_____ and be reconciled (Matt 5:24).
     How can I demonstrate the forgiveness of God and encourage a reasonable solution to this conflict?

3. The Foundational G: the G_____ of Christ
   Christ Jesus came into the world to save sinners (1 Tim. 1:15).

4. How do we respond to conflict?
   - _____ responses: Peace-faking
   - _____ responses: Peace-breaking
   - _____ responses: Peacemaking

Personal Peacemaking	Overlook an offense (Prov. 19:11)
	Reconciliation (Matt. 5:23–24)
	Negotiation (Phil. 2:3–4)

Assisted Peacemaking	Mediation (Matt. 18:16)
	Arbitration (1 Cor. 6:1–8)
	Accountability (Matt. 18:17–20)

Key Principle: Conflict is an opportunity.

What Do You Think?

1. Watch the "Gossiping about Gossip" Peacemaker Parable. Which Slippery Slope responses were people using? Which of the Four G's did they miss? How might the conversation have sounded if they had used all of the Four G's and the peacemaking zone of the Slippery Slope?

2. Individually or in pairs, silently read one or two of the following passages and then explain to the group or to your partner what Slippery Slope responses people used, and whether those responses were wise or foolish. (After discussion, compare your answers with those on page 63.)
    a) Abram, Sarai and Hagar (Gen. 16:1–6)
    b) Joseph and Potiphar's wife (Gen. 39:1–18)
    c) Joseph and his brothers (Gen. 37:17–28; 45:1–7; 50:15–21)
    d) King Saul and David (1 Sam. 18:1–11; 19:9–12)
    e) Daniel (Dan. 1:1–16)
    f) The apostles (Acts 6:1–7)
    g) Saul (Paul) and Barnabas (Acts 9:20–28)
    h) Paul (1 Cor. 5:1–5; 2 Cor. 2:5–11; see Matt. 18:15–20)

3. What Slippery Slope responses did God model while resolving mankind's conflict with him? Which of the Four G's did he model? (After discussion, compare your responses to the answer on page 63.)

4. What responses on the Slippery Slope come most naturally to you? Why? How do your responses usually affect the people around you? Give an example.

5. Which of the Four G's do you do most naturally? Least naturally? How would your response to conflict change if you really saw conflict as an opportunity to glorify God, grow to be like Christ, serve others, and demonstrate the reconciling power of the gospel?

Pray for One Another

My Next Step

When I face conflict this week, I will note how I am tempted to be a peace-faker or a peace-breaker, and I'll ask God to help me be a peacemaker by living out the Four G's.

Session Two
Live at Peace

MEMORY VERSE
A new command I give you: Love one another. As I have loved you, so you must love one another. By this all men will know that you are my disciples, if you love one another (John 13:34–35).

KEY PRINCIPLE
Living at peace is a key to our Christian witness.

Suggested Weekly Reading in *The Peacemaker*
- Day 1 – Pages 43–45
- Day 2 – Pages 46–50
- Day 3 – Pages 50–51
- Day 4 – Pages 51–53
- Day 5 – Pages 53–57
- Optional – Pages 270–275

THOUGHTS AND QUESTIONS
Thoughts or questions that come to my mind as I read, which I can share with my group:

_____
_____
_____
_____
_____
_____
_____
_____
_____
_____
_____

Part 1 – Glorify God
How can I please and honor God in this situation?

Group Study

Icebreaker

Learning Together (Video)

1. The three dimensions of peace.

- Peace with _____.
  God was pleased to have all his fullness dwell in [Christ], and through him to reconcile to himself all things . . . by making peace through his blood, shed on the cross (Col. 1:19–20).

- Peace with _____—unity.
  If it is possible, as far as it depends on you, live at peace with everyone (Rom. 12:18).

- Peace within _____.
  The fruit of righteousness will be peace; the effect of righteousness will be quietness and confidence forever (Isa. 32:17).

If only you had paid attention to my commands, your peace would have been like a river, your righteousness like the waves of the sea (Isa. 48:18).

Inner peace is a by-product of being right with God and others.

2. Jesus' _____ depends on peace and unity in the church.
   A new command I give you: Love one another. As I have loved you, so you must love one another. All men will know that you are my disciples if you love one another (John 13:34–35; see John 17:20–23).

3. Jesus calls us to seek reconciliation _____ of worship.
   Therefore, if you are offering your gift at the altar and there remember that your brother has something against you, leave your gift there in front of the altar. First go and be reconciled to your brother; then come and offer your gift (Matt. 5:23–24).

4. Peacemaking shows that we take the _____ seriously.
   As a prisoner for the Lord, then, I urge you to live a life worthy of the calling you have received. Be completely humble and gentle; be patient, bearing with one another in love. Make every effort to keep the unity of the Spirit through the bond of peace (Eph. 4:1–3).

5. Even our _____ should be resolved within the church!
   If any of you has a dispute with another, dare he take it before the ungodly for judgment instead of before the saints? ... If you have disputes about such matters, appoint as judges even men of little account in the church! (1 Cor. 6:1–8).

Key Principle: Living at peace is a key to our Christian witness.

What Do You Think?

(If your meetings are running too long, divide into smaller groups of 3 or 4 during the discussion time, so all can share their thoughts in less time.)

1. Watch the "Repentance" Peacemaker Parable. The "Golden Result" (a corollary of the Golden Rule) says that *people will usually treat us the same way we treat them.* How was this principle illustrated in this situation? How could this principle help you to have a positive witness for Christ even in the midst of conflict?

2. What is it that sometimes keeps you from being at peace with God, with others, or within yourself?

3. Why does Satan love to see Christians in conflict? How does he stir up conflict in the church? (See pages 50–51 in *The Peacemaker.*)

4. Why do you think God commands us to seek reconciliation ahead of worship and to resolve lawsuits against others in the church instead of in court? Why do you think many of us ignore these commands?

5. Describe a situation in which a Christian's response to conflict (no names or identifying facts) diminished his or her Christian witness. Describe another situation in which a believer's efforts to seek peace and reconciliation gave witness to the love and power of Christ.

Pray for One Another

My Next Step

If I can think of anyone who may have something against me, I will go and seek reconciliation this week. If it is a difficult situation, I will begin praying and preparing to approach that person before this study is over.

Session Three
Conflict Starts in the Heart

MEMORY VERSE
What causes fights and quarrels among you? Don't they come from your desires that battle within you? (James 4:1)

KEY PRINCIPLE
God uses conflict to reveal our idols.

Suggested Weekly Reading in *The Peacemaker*
- Day 1 – Pages 100–103
- Day 2 – Pages 103–106
- Day 3 – Pages 106–109
- Day 4 – Pages 109–112
- Day 5 – Pages 112–115

THOUGHTS AND QUESTIONS
Thoughts or questions that come to my mind as I read, which I can share with my group:

Part 2 – Get the Log Out of Your Eye
How can I show Jesus' work in me by taking responsibility for my contribution to this conflict?

Group Study

Icebreaker

Learning Together (Video)

1. The progression of an idol:

   - I _____.

   - I _____—the birth of an idol.
     But those who trust in idols, who say to images, "You are our gods," will be turned back in utter shame (Isa. 42:17).

     An idol is anything apart from God that we depend on to be happy, fulfilled, or secure. It is something other than God that we set our hearts on (*Luke 12:29*), that rules us (*Eph. 5:5*), or that we trust, fear, or serve (*Isa. 42:17; Luke 12:4–5; Matt. 6:24*). Given its controlling effect on our lives, an idol may be referred to as a "functional god."

   - I _____.
     Brothers, do not slander one another. Anyone who speaks against his brother or judges him speaks against the law and judges it (James 4:11).

   - I _____.
     Now Cain said to his brother Abel, "Let's go out to the field." And while they were in the field, Cain attacked his brother Abel and killed him (Gen. 4:8; see Prov. 27:15).

2. Expose idols by asking "_____" questions.
   Let us examine our ways and test them, and let us return to the LORD (Lam. 3:40).

   - With what am I preoccupied?

   - How would I complete the statement: "If only _____, then I would be happy, fulfilled, and secure"?

- When a certain desire is not met, do I feel frustration, anxiety, resentment, bitterness, anger, or depression?

3. The cure for an idolatrous heart:

- _____ and receive God's refreshing forgiveness.
  Repent, then, and turn to God, so that your sins may be wiped out, that times of refreshing may come from the Lord (Acts 3:19).

- Worship and _____ yourself in the Lord.
  Delight yourself in the LORD and he will give you the desires of your heart (Ps. 37:4).

> Key Principle: God uses conflict to reveal our idols.

What Do You Think?

1. Watch the "Word Pictures" Peacemaker Parable. As you watch the sketch, make a note of the desires that have grown into controlling demands, and how people have judged and punished each other.

2. What desires do you have that sometimes grow into controlling demands or idols that trigger or aggravate conflict?

3. How do you judge and punish those around you when your idols are not being satisfied? How does your behavior affect others?

4. What attributes, promises, or activities of God can you celebrate and depend on for happiness, fulfillment, and security, in order to diminish the appeal and power of idolatrous desires?

5. What could you and others in your group do to diminish the influence of hidden idolatry within your families and your church?

Pray for One Another

My Next Step

I will think of someone who has been affected by one of my idols. I will write a brief but clear description of the progression of that idol (the initial desire, why it became a demand, and how I judged and punished the other person). Next week I will learn how to use confession to cast down this idol and repair the damage it has caused.

Session Four
Confession Brings Freedom

MEMORY VERSE

He who conceals his sins does not prosper, but whoever confesses and renounces them finds mercy (Prov. 28:13).

KEY PRINCIPLE

Confession brings freedom.

Suggested Weekly Reading in *The Peacemaker*
- Day 1 – Pages 117–119
- Day 2 – Pages 119–123
- Day 3 – Pages 123–126
- Day 4 – Pages 126–130
- Day 5 – Pages 131–136
- Optional – Pages 276–278

THOUGHTS AND QUESTIONS

Thoughts or questions that come to my mind as I read, which I can share with my group:

Part 2 – Get the Log Out of Your Eye
How can I show Jesus' work in me by taking responsibility for my contribution to this conflict?

Group Study

Icebreaker

Learning Together (Video)

The Seven A's of Confession

- A _____ everyone involved (Luke 19:8).

- A _____ if, but, and maybe (Ps. 51).

- A _____ specifically.

Sinful desires/idols
- Inherently sinful cravings or attitudes, such as pride, lust, greed, or hatred.

- Good things that we want too much, without which we feel we cannot be content, fulfilled, secure, or happy.

Sinful words
- Harsh, reckless, or worthless words.

- Grumbling and complaining.

- Falsehood—any deception or twisting of the truth.

- Gossip—revealing or discussing personal information about others with people who are not part of the problem or the solution.

- Slander—speaking false and malicious words.

Sinful actions
- Not keeping your word.

- Not respecting authority.

- Not treating others as you want to be treated.

- A _____ the hurt. Express sincere sorrow for the way you affected others.

- A _____ the consequences (Luke 15:19; Luke 19:8).

- A _____ (change) your behavior (Eph. 4:22–32).

- A _____ for forgiveness and allow time (Gen. 50:17).

> Key Principle: Confession brings freedom.

What Do You Think?

1. Watch the "I'm Really Sorry" Peacemaker Parable. What Slippery Slope responses did the couple use? Which of the Seven A's of Confession did the husband fail to follow?

2. Why do we often find it so difficult to confess our wrongs? What are some of the ways we minimize or avoid admitting our sin?

3. Which step in the Seven A's of Confession is the most difficult for you to do sincerely and thoroughly? Why?

4. How can your celebrating and meditating on God's grace and forgiveness help you to confess your sins more easily and quickly?

5. Describe the most encouraging and effective confession you have ever received, given, or heard about within your church. What made it so compelling?

Pray for One Another

My Next Step

Referring to the "progression of an idol" description I wrote in My Next Step last week, I will write a complete "Seven A's" confession of how my desires and actions have affected the other person. I will go to that person this week and make a sincere and thorough confession, asking God to bring about a genuine reconciliation.

Session Five
Just Between the Two of You

MEMORY VERSE
Brothers, if someone is caught in a sin, you who are spiritual should restore him gently (Gal. 6:1).

KEY PRINCIPLE
Constructive correction is a sign of genuine love.

Suggested Weekly Reading in *The Peacemaker*
- Day 1 – Pages 139–142
- Day 2 – Pages 143–148
- Day 3 – Pages 148–152
- Day 4 – Pages 152–155
- Day 5 – Pages 155–160

THOUGHTS AND QUESTIONS
Thoughts or questions that come to my mind as I read, which I can share with my group:

_____
_____
_____
_____
_____
_____
_____
_____
_____
_____
_____
_____
_____

Part 3—Gently Restore
How can I lovingly serve others by helping them take responsibility for their contribution to this conflict?

Group Study

Icebreaker

Learning Together (Video)

1. God calls us to lovingly _____ one another.
   If your brother sins against you, go and show him his fault, just between the two of you. If he listens to you, you have won your brother over (Matt. 18:15).

2. Correcting means more than _____ .
   What do you think? If a man owns a hundred sheep, and one of them wanders away, will he not leave the ninety-nine on the hills and go to look for the one that wandered off? (Matt. 18:12; see Matt. 18:21–35; Gal. 6:1)

3. Sooner or later, talk _____-to-_____ (see Gen. 32–33; 50:15–21; 2 Sam. 14:24; Matt. 5:23–24).

4. Go when someone's sins are too _____ to overlook.

- Is it dishonoring God? (Rom. 2:21–24)

- Is it damaging your relationship?

- Is it hurting others (or you)? (Luke 17:2–3; 1 Cor. 5:6)

- Is it hurting the offender?
  My brothers, if one of you should wander from the truth and someone should bring him back, remember this: Whoever turns a sinner from the error of his way will save him from death and cover over a multitude of sins (James 5:19–20).

5. Special considerations:

- First get the log out of your own eye.

- Approach non-Christians gently.

- Respect those in authority.

- Deal cautiously with abuse.

- Go tentatively ... go repeatedly.

Key Principle: Constructive correction is a sign of genuine love.

What Do You Think?

1. Watch the "Slippery Slope Denial" Peacemaker Parable. What Slippery Slope response was the mother using? Why was the offense in this situation too serious to overlook? What would probably happen if the mother failed to go and talk with the other woman?

2. Before you did this study, what thoughts or feelings came to mind when you heard the word "correction"? Why is correction often viewed as being a negative rather than a positive activity?

3. What damage can occur if you correct others for selfish reasons or in a clumsy manner? What benefits result from seeking to correct and restore someone out of genuine love and in a carefully planned way?

4. Some people in the church tend to "over-correct" (confront others too eagerly and quickly), while others tend to "under-correct" (avoid offering correction even when it is truly needed). What excuses do we often use to justify these tendencies? What biblical passages or principles will help us to avoid these extremes?

5. When and how is it appropriate to involve other people in a conflict before we talk personally with the person who is at odds with us? What is the benefit of eventually talking face-to-face?

Pray for One Another

My Next Step

I will evaluate my "correction inclination" by reflecting on recent conflicts in my life and discerning whether I am inclined to "over-correct" or "under-correct." I will identify three characteristics of Christ that I can imitate to learn how to correct and restore others in a more loving and timely manner.

Session Six
Take One or Two Others Along

Part 3 – Gently Restore
How can I lovingly serve others by helping them take responsibility for their contribution to this conflict?

MEMORY VERSE
But if he will not listen, take one or two others along, so that "every matter may be established by the testimony of two or three witnesses." If he refuses to listen to them, tell it to the church; and if he refuses to listen even to the church, treat him as you would a pagan or a tax collector (Matt. 18:16–17).

KEY PRINCIPLE
Discipline is God's gift and blessing to the church.

Suggested Weekly Reading in *The Peacemaker*
- Day 1 – Pages 185–187
- Day 2 – Pages 187–190
- Day 3 – Pages 191–193
- Day 4 – Pages 193–196
- Day 5 – Pages 197–199
- Optional – Pages 279–286

THOUGHTS AND QUESTIONS
Thoughts or questions that come to my mind as I read, which I can share with my group:

_____
_____
_____
_____
_____
_____
_____
_____

Small Group Study

Group Study

Icebreaker

Learning Together (Video)

1. Step One: Overlook minor offenses (Prov. 19:11).

2. Step Two: Talk privately (Matt. 18:15).

3. Step Three: Take _____ or _____ others along.
   But if he will not listen, take one or two others along, so that "every matter may be established by the testimony of two or three witnesses"(Matt. 18:16).

   - To mediate or arbitrate (1 Cor. 6:1–8)

   - To encourage self-control and courtesy

   - To ask questions, clarify facts

   - To counsel and admonish by God's Word

   - To observe conduct and report to church or churches

4. Step Four: Tell it to the _____.
   If he refuses to listen to them, tell it to the church (Matt. 18:17a).

5. Step Five: Treat the other person as a _____.
   And if he refuses to listen even to the church, treat him as you would a pagan or a tax collector (Matt. 18:17b).

   - To convict and restore those who stray (1 Cor. 5:1–13)

"Nothing is so cruel as the tenderness that consigns another to his sin. Nothing can be more compassionate than the severe rebuke that calls a brother back from the path of sin."
– Dietrich Bonhoeffer, *Life Together*

- To guard others from stumbling
  Don't you know that a little yeast works through the whole batch of dough? (1 Cor. 5:6; see 1 Tim. 5:20; Titus 3:10–11) [Galatians 5:9]

- To protect God's name (Rom. 2:24)

6. Step Six: Forgive and _____ the repentant.
   What do you think? If a man owns a hundred sheep, and one of them wanders away, will he not leave the ninety-nine on the hills and go to look for the one that wandered off? And if he finds it, I tell you the truth, he is happier about that one sheep than about the ninety-nine that did not wander off. In the same way your Father in heaven is not willing that any of these little ones should be lost (Matt. 18:12–14; see 2 Cor. 2:5–11).

> **Key Principle: Discipline is God's gift and blessing to the church.**

What Do You Think?

1. Watch the "Virtual Confrontation" Peacemaker Parable. Why do we often prefer to deal with conflict through email, letters, or a telephone? What do we lose when we fail to talk in person?

2. Describe a situation from your experience in which a spiritually mature third party might have helped to resolve a conflict more quickly or effectively. How might that person have helped?

3. Many churches are reluctant to get involved in members' conflicts, as commanded in Matthew 18:15–16 and 1 Corinthians 6:1–8, and even more reluctant to exercise formal church discipline, as commanded in Matthew 18:17. Why do you think this is?

4. Reread Dietrich Bonhoeffer's statement on the previous page. Describe a time when a church's failure to get involved in a conflict seemed like "tenderness" but actually "consigned another to his sin," or a time when a church's discipline may have seemed "severe" to some people and yet "called someone back from the path of sin."

5. What might happen (both short-term and long-term) if more churches practiced loving, redemptive accountability and discipline? What would they need to guard against? What specific steps could you take to support loving discipline in your church?

Pray for One Another

My Next Step

I will think about a time where I had the wrong attitude in confronting someone—condemning rather than restoring. Using the guidelines from Session Four, I will prepare a confession related to this situation. Then I will go to that person this week and make a sincere confession. Later (probably not during the same conversation), if God opens the door, I will make another attempt to "gently restore" this person using a more loving and redemptive attitude, keeping the gospel at the center of the conversation.

Session Seven
Forgive as God Forgave You

Part 4 – Go and Be Reconciled
How can I demonstrate the forgiveness of God and encourage a reasonable solution to this conflict?

MEMORY VERSE

Therefore, if you are offering your gift at the altar and there remember that your brother has something against you, leave your gift there in front of the altar. First go and be reconciled to your brother; then come and offer your gift (Matt. 5:23–24).

KEY PRINCIPLE
Our forgiveness shows what we think of God's forgiveness.

Suggested Weekly Reading in *The Peacemaker*
- Day 1 – Pages 201–206
- Day 2 – Pages 206–210
- Day 3 – Pages 210–213
- Day 4 – Pages 213–218
- Day 5 – Pages 219–223

THOUGHTS AND QUESTIONS
Thoughts or questions that come to my mind as I read, which I can share with my group:

_____
_____
_____
_____
_____
_____
_____
_____
_____
_____
_____
_____

Small Group Study

Group Study

Icebreaker

Learning Together (Video)

1. You _____ forgive in your own strength.

2. Forgiveness is neither a feeling, nor forgetting, nor excusing.

3. Sin creates a _____ that must be paid.

   He himself bore our sins in his body on the tree, so that we might die to sins and live for righteousness; by his wounds you have been healed (1 Pet. 2:24).

   Forgive us our debts, as we also have forgiven our debtors (Matt. 6:12).

   - Will you _____ payments?

   - Or _____ payments?

4. Forgiveness is a _____ modeled after God's forgiveness.

   Bear with each other and forgive whatever grievances you may have against one another. Forgive as the Lord forgave you (Col. 3:13).

   Love . . . keeps no record of wrongs (1 Cor. 13:4–5).

"In response to God's love for me and in reliance on his grace, I forgive you. Specifically, with God's help ...

- I promise I will not _____ on this incident."

- I promise I will not _____ up this incident and use it against you."

- I promise I will not _____ to others about this incident."

- I promise I will not allow this incident to _____ between us or _____ our personal relationship."

5. God's forgiveness _____ our forgiveness.
   Then the master called the servant in. "You wicked servant," he said, "I canceled all that debt of yours because you begged me to. Shouldn't you have had mercy on your fellow servant just as I had on you?" (Matt. 18:32–33)

> **Key Principle: Our forgiveness shows what we think of God's forgiveness.**

What Do You Think?

1. Watch the "Forgive You, No Problem" Peacemaker Parable. What did Andrew really mean when he said, "I forgive you, no problem"? What are some other ways that people wrongly understand and live out forgiveness?

2. Who is the most forgiving person you know? How does he or she make you or others feel forgiven?

3. Reflect on the statement, "Sin creates a debt that must be paid." When others sin against you, what are some ways that you are tempted to "take payments" on their debt? How could you deliberately "make payments" on their debt?

Small Group Bible Study

4. Which of the "I promise" statements from the previous page do you feel least like making or keeping? Why? How can focusing on the forgiveness God offers through the gospel help you to make and keep that promise?

5. Some churches are viewed as being unforgiving. How does that affect the willingness of members to confess and seek help with their sins? How could your church cultivate a reputation for being forgiving? How would that affect your people and your witness for Christ?

Pray for One Another

My Next Step

If I can think of someone I need to forgive (or forgave in a superficial way in the past), I will go to that person and affirm my forgiveness, specifically making the four promises and explaining that they are modeled after the forgiveness God has given to me through Christ.

I will also pray about becoming involved with the Peacemaking Team at my church.

Session Eight
Overcome Evil with Good

Part 4 – Go and Be Reconciled
How can I demonstrate the forgiveness of God and encourage a reasonable solution to this conflict?

MEMORY VERSE
If your enemy is hungry, feed him; if he is thirsty, give him something to drink. In doing this, you will heap burning coals on his head. Do not be overcome by evil, but overcome evil with good (Rom. 12:20–21).

KEY PRINCIPLE
Overcome evil with good.

Suggested Weekly Reading in *The Peacemaker*
- Day 1 – Pages 247–249
- Day 2 – Pages 249–250
- Day 3 – Pages 250–253
- Day 4 – Pages 253–256
- Day 5 – Pages 259–261
- Optional – Pages 263–269

THOUGHTS AND QUESTIONS
Thoughts or questions that come to my mind as I read, which I can share with my group:

_____
_____
_____
_____
_____
_____
_____
_____
_____
_____
_____
_____
_____

Group Study
Icebreaker

Learning Together (Video)

1. We have _____ weapons.

   For though we live in the world, we do not wage war as the world does. The weapons we fight with are not the weapons of the world. On the contrary, they have divine power to demolish strongholds. We demolish arguments and every pretension that sets itself up against the know-ledge of God, and we take captive every thought to make it obedient to Christ (2 Cor. 10:3–5).

2. Control your _____.

   Bless those who persecute you; bless and do not curse (Rom. 12:14).

3. Seek godly _____ —and listen to them!

   Rejoice with those who rejoice; mourn with those who mourn. Live in harmony with one another. Do not be proud, but be willing to associate with people of low position. Do not be conceited (Rom. 12:15–16).

4. Keep doing what is _____.
   Be careful to do what is right in the eyes of everybody (Rom. 12:17; cf. 1 Pet. 2:12, 15; 3:15–16; 1 Sam. 24:16–20).

5. Recognize your _____.

   If it is possible, as far as it depends on you, live at peace with everyone. Do not take revenge, my friends, but leave room for God's wrath, for it is written: "It is mine to avenge; I will repay," says the Lord (Rom. 12:18–19).

6. The ultimate weapon: deliberate, focused _____.
   On the contrary: "If your enemy is hungry, feed him; if he is thirsty, give him something to drink. In doing this, you will heap burning coals on his head." Do not be overcome by evil, but overcome evil with good (Rom. 12:20–21; see Luke 6:27–31).

   - Protects you from your own bitterness and resentment.

   - May help to bring the other person to repentance.

> **Key Principle: Overcome evil with good.**

*Blessed are the peacemakers,
for they will be called the sons of God (Matt. 5:9).*

What Do You Think?

1. Watch "Why Not Rather Be Wronged" from Peacemaker Parables (a conversation between a lawyer and his client). Describe a time when you saw a Christian do something that was so consistent with Scripture and so different from the world that it puzzled or amazed others.

2. Describe a prolonged or difficult conflict situation in which you finally gave up on doing what the Bible teaches and started to use worldly techniques to get what you wanted. How did it turn out?

3. What spiritual weapon or peacemaking principle might you have applied in that situation to better glorify God, serve other people and grow to be like Christ?

4. Describe a time when you or someone in your church kept doing what was right during a conflict in spite of great temptation to give up on God's ways and use the weapons of the world. How did the other person respond? How did such conduct honor the Lord?

5. Describe a time when you or someone else responded to an opponent by living out Romans 12:20–21 ("if your enemy is hungry…"). How did such behavior affect others? How did it bring glory to God?

Be sure to watch Ken Sande's five-minute closing to the study now!

Pray for One Another

My Next Step

I will ask God to bring to mind a person who has been so difficult to deal with that I have been tempted to give up on him or her. I will write a plan on how to apply the six principles in this section to that conflict.

As I come to the end of this study, real life suggests that I will forget much of what I have learned. Therefore, I will develop a long-term plan for growing and serving as a peacemaker by considering the options on the following pages.

Next Steps
Growing and Serving as a Peacemaker

Do not merely listen to the word, and so deceive yourselves.
Do what it says! (James 1:22)

Step 1: Continue Your Study

Step 2: Share Your Story

Step 3: Teach the Principles

Step 4: Be a Part of the Peacemaking Team

Step 1: Continue to Study and Apply Peacemaking

- As a group, consider going through the four optional sessions included in this study. If you've enjoyed the lessons so far, you'll appreciate the additional concepts these sessions cover.
- If you haven't yet done so, read The Peacemaker. This book is the foundational resource on biblical peacemaking, and any additional study on the topic of peacemaking should include it.
- Visit www.Peacemaker.net and subscribe to the free resources such as the PeaceMeal e-devotional and Peacemaker Magazine. These resources will stimulate your growth as a peacemaker.
- While you are visiting our website, browse through the other peacemaking resources available—resources for marriages, women, children, business, pastors... and much more!
- Keep applying peacemaking principles in your life. Some ways include:
    - List the two peacemaking skills presented in this study that you would most like to improve in the next three months.

    - Share your list with two people who are close to you, and ask them to pray for you and regularly ask about your progress. Pray daily that God will give you opportunities to practice these skills, and keep a journal of your progress.
    - Write the names of one or two people with whom you would like to resolve a conflict or reconcile more fully (perhaps by practicing the skills listed above).

- Use the *Peacemaker Workbook* (available through the bookstore at www.Peacemaker.net) to develop a specific reconciliation plan.
- Share your plan with a close friend who will pray for you and encourage your progress.

Step 2: Share What God Has Done in Your Life

In Scripture, reconciliation is always a reason to celebrate. When a single sinner is reconciled to God, all of heaven rejoices (Luke 15:7). And how about the father of the prodigal son, who held a feast when his son repented (Luke 15:20–24)?

> **In Scripture, reconciliation is always a reason to celebrate!**

Maybe you've had a dramatic reconciliation experience in the course of this study. Or perhaps God simply used these materials to change your own heart. In either case, it's a significant evidence of God's grace. Like the examples from Scripture, celebrate it and share it with others! Here are a few ideas on how you can do this:

- Hold a special small group session for the express purpose of celebrating what God has done in your midst. Gather your families and even invite people with whom you've been reconciled! Then take time for each person to share what he/she has seen God do as a result of this study.
- Share what you've learned with your family and friends.
- Tell your story to your pastor as an encouragement to him. Perhaps it would also be appropriate for you to share with the whole congregation.

Other people are struggling every day to persevere in peacemaking, and when they hear you tell how God has helped you to live out the gospel, they will be encouraged to keep on seeking to do the same in their lives. So please don't keep your story to yourself. Share it!

Step 3: Teach Peacemaking to Someone Else

The best way to make sure you understand the material is to teach it to someone else. Here are a few simple ways:
- Invite one or two friends out for coffee or lunch, and walk them through the basic principles of peacemaking, as summarized in this study guide or in the Peacemaking Principles pamphlet.
- Use The Young Peacemaker curriculum to teach peacemaking to your children and/or other children in your church or neighborhood.
- Volunteer to lead another group through this study, either in your church, neighborhood, or workplace.

Step 4: Consider Being a Part of Your Church's Peacemaking Team

Even the best teaching eventually fades away. Therefore, five years from now, if peacemaking is to be a vital part of your church, then a Peacemaking Team needs to be established today. Like any of the other ministries in your church (e.g., evangelism, missions, children's ministry, etc.) someone besides the pastor needs to own it and keep it going. Perhaps you are one of those people! The team would provide the context for you to:

> **If peacemaking is going to be a part of your church in five years, then a Peacemaking Team needs to be established today.**

- Pursue further formal training in peacemaking (e.g., Conflict Coaching/Mediation or Certification as a Christian conciliator) and attend the annual Peacemaker Conference.
- Teach peacemaking to new members, missions teams, engaged couples—anyone in your church who missed this round of peacemaking teaching.
- Walk along with and assist other church members who are in conflict, giving guidance and counsel based on the skills you have learned.

Thank you once again for your commitment to this study and to the principles you've learned. May God richly bless both you and your church as you continue to seek to respond to conflict biblically.

Optional Small Group Study Sessions

Optional Session A
Trust in the Lord and Do Good

If keeping in sequence with *The Peacemaker*, this session would logically fit after Session 2.

MEMORY VERSE
Commit your way to the LORD; trust in him and he will do this: He will make your righteousness shine like the dawn, the justice of your cause like the noonday sun (Psalm 37:5–6).

KEY PRINCIPLE
Trusting God frees us to respond to conflict biblically.

Suggested Weekly Reading in *The Peacemaker*
- Day 1 – Pages 59–62
- Day 2 – Pages 62–65
- Day 3 – Pages 65–66
- Day 4 – Pages 67–70
- Day 5 – Pages 70–72
- Optional – Pages 287–288

THOUGHTS AND QUESTIONS
Thoughts or questions that come to my mind as I read, which I can share with my group:

_____
_____
_____
_____
_____
_____
_____
_____
_____
_____
_____

Small Group Study

Part 1 – Glorify God
How can I please and honor God in this situation?

Group Study

Icebreaker

Learning Together (Video)

1. Faithful peacemaking requires a _____.

- God is _____—supreme, unlimited, and totally in control.
  I make known the end from the beginning, from ancient times, what is still to come. I say: My purpose will stand, and I will do all that I please (Isa. 46:10; see Dan. 2:20–22).

- God is not only all-powerful, but also _____—He is for us!
  One thing God has spoken, two things have I heard: that you, O God, are strong, and that you, O Lord, are loving (Ps. 62:11–12).

- Therefore, nothing happens by "_____"—not even suffering or conflict!
  Are not two sparrows sold for a penny? Yet not one of them will fall to the ground apart from the will of your Father. And even the very hairs of your head are all numbered. So don't be afraid; you are worth more than many sparrows (Matt. 10:29–30; see 1 Pet. 2:20–23).

- Trusting does not require _____ everything.
  The secret things belong to the Lord our God, but the things revealed belong to us and to our children forever, that we may follow all the words of this law (Deut. 29:29).

2. The path of trust has been _____.

- Joseph (Gen. 45:5; 50:20)

- David (Psalm 37:5–6)

- Shadrach, Meshach, and Abednego (Dan. 3:16–18)

- Peter (Acts. 4:27–29)

- Paul (2 Tim. 1:12)

- Jesus (Matt. 26:42)

3. Trust is a _____ based on faith.

- "Why me, Lord!"   Meaning, "This isn't fair!"
  vs.
- "Why, Lord?"   Meaning, "Please show me all that I
                         need to know, so I can cooperate with you."

Key Principle: Trusting God frees us to respond to conflict biblically.

What Do You Think?

1. Name someone in your life who you deeply trust. What makes this person trustworthy?

2. In what situations do you find it most difficult to trust God? Why?

3. Think of a conflict in which you did not trust God and follow his ways. What was the result? Think of a situation when you did trust God and follow his ways. What was the result?

4. What does not trusting God in the midst of conflict look like? (What kinds of things do we think, feel, say, and do?) What does trusting God in the midst of conflict look like? Share real-life examples.

5. What characteristics of God encourage you to trust him? How can focusing on these characteristics strengthen your ability to respond to conflict in a confident and constructive way?

Pray for One Another

My Next Step
I will read the case study below to see how I can accelerate my growth as a peacemaker.

I will think of a situation in which I am finding it difficult to trust God and obey his commands. I will talk with a spiritually mature friend and prayerfully write a description of what I think, say, and do, as I trust God with that situation.

Accelerate Your Growth as a Peacemaker
The more you practice and apply the principles presented in this study, the more quickly you will learn how to be an effective peacemaker. For example, imagine that you received the following message from a friend.

> *I wish I had never agreed to serve on our missions committee! One of the other committee members is so irritating! Pat delights in using cutting humor and seems to look for ways to ridicule others' ideas and suggestions —especially mine.*
>
> *When Pat disagreed with me on a financial issue during last night's meeting, I finally lost my patience. Knowing that he is self-conscious about not going to college, I said something like, "I can see why these figures are hard for you to understand, Pat, but if you just had a little more education, it would all add up." He just sat there, stunned, and the rest of the group moved on with the discussion. It was awkward. I felt sort of sorry about what I had said, but I also think he had it coming.*
>
> *This morning I found a letter from Pat under my door—he must have delivered it late last night. The letter goes on for two pages harshly accusing me of all sorts of wrongs. I can see why he is angry with me for belittling him in front of others, but he has made all sorts of other accusations that are exaggerated or completely untrue. He concludes by saying I am unfit to serve on the missions committee. And he had the nerve to send a copy to the committee chairman!*

> *I'm torn between writing him a letter pointing out how he brought this on himself, or discussing it on the phone. What do you think I should do?*

It's tempting for us to quickly respond to this kind of a question from a friend by saying, "Well, have you thought about trying …?" But peacemaking is a reflective process that goes beyond giving a simple piece of advice or making an appeal to common sense. It involves thoughtful, detailed reflection on the Scriptures, using tools like the Four G's.

A peacemaker could help this missions committee member turn an ugly spat into an opportunity to respond to conflict biblically.

Offering detailed, biblical advice doesn't come naturally, but any committed Christian who is willing to practice can learn to do it. Can you imagine a top athlete practicing only on the playing field and only during actual games? Of course not! But that's often what we do with peacemaking! Becoming a skilled peacemaker requires regular practice before you get on the "field of conflict," and you can use other resources available from Peacemaker Ministries to do just that. Three additional case studies (like the one on the previous page) are available online, and there are many other tools available that complement and build on what you have learned in the group study.

Many other excellent resources on biblical peacemaking are available at https://pm.training/.

50 Trust in the Lord and Do Good

Optional Session B
Is This Really Worth Fighting Over?

If keeping in sequence with *The Peacemaker*, this session would logically fit after Session A.

MEMORY VERSE
First take the plank out of your own eye, and then you will see clearly to remove the speck from your brother's eye (Matt. 7:5).

KEY PRINCIPLE
A gracious, gentle attitude can prevent most conflicts.

Suggested Weekly Reading in *The Peacemaker*
- Day 1 – Pages 75–78
- Day 2 – Pages 79–83
- Day 3 – Pages 83–90
- Day 4 – Pages 90–91
- Day 5 – Pages 92–98

THOUGHTS AND QUESTIONS
Thoughts or questions that come to my mind as I read, which I can share with my group:

___

OPTIONAL SESSION

Part 2 – Get the Log Out of Your Eye

How can I show Jesus' work in me by taking responsibility for my contribution to this conflict?

Small Group Study

Group Study

Icebreaker

Learning Together (Video)

1. Two kinds of logs to remove:

- A critical, negative _____ that leads to unnecessary conflict.

- Actual sinful _____ or _____.

2. God calls us to _____ minor offenses.
A man's wisdom gives him patience; it is to his glory to overlook an offense (Prov. 19:11).

- Why? To imitate the Lord (Ps. 103:8–10).

- When?
  o If the offense is not dishonoring God.
  o If your relationship has not been permanently damaged.
  o If others are not being hurt.

3. Check your _____—and change it (Phil. 4:4–9).

- _____ in the Lord always.
Rejoice in the Lord always. I will say it again: Rejoice! (Phil. 4:4)

- Let your _____ be evident to all.
Let your gentleness be evident to all. The Lord is near (Phil. 4:5).

- _____ anxiety with prayer.
Do not be anxious about anything, but in everything, by prayer and petition, with thanksgiving, present your requests to God. And the peace of God, which transcends all understanding, will guard your hearts and your minds in Christ Jesus (Phil. 4:6–7).

- See things as they _____.
  Finally, brothers, whatever is true, whatever is noble, whatever is right, whatever is pure, whatever is lovely, whatever is admirable—if anything is excellent or praiseworthy—think about such things (Phil. 4:8).

- _____ what you've learned.
  Whatever you have learned or received or heard from me, or seen in me—put it into practice. And the God of peace will be with you (Phil. 4:9).

4. Count the _____.
Settle matters quickly with your adversary who is taking you to court ... or he may hand you over to the judge ... and you may be thrown into prison (Matt. 5:25–26).

> **Key Principle: A gracious, gentle attitude can prevent most conflicts.**

Small Group Study

What Do You Think?

1. Watch the "Think on These Things" Peacemaker Parable. What kind of "log" did the woman have in her eye? What is it about her situation that makes her focus on her co-worker's faults? How did focusing on his virtues change the course of this conflict?

2. Think of a type of minor offense that you find difficult to overlook. Why is it so difficult? How would you and the people around you be affected if God enabled you to be more gracious, gentle, and inclined to overlook that type of offense?

3. Reflect on a conflict you have experienced. What more could you have rejoiced about in the midst of that situation? (See pages 84–85 in *The Peacemaker*.)

4. What costs of conflict have you forgotten to take into account when deciding how to respond to someone who offended you? What is the biggest "conflict price tag" you've ever paid?

5. Every church has a peacemaking "culture," which is a combination of its attitudes, expectations, habits, and unwritten rules for dealing with conflict. What aspects of your church's culture promote peace? What aspect undermines peace? What can you do to improve your church's peacemaking culture?

Pray for One Another

My Next Step

I will do an "attitude checkup" (Phil. 4:4–9) and count the cost of an existing conflict to decide whether I should pursue the matter or overlook the offense. (If I have no present conflicts, I will evaluate a past conflict to decide whether it was worth pursuing.)

Optional Session C
Speak the Truth in Love

If keeping in sequence with The Peacemaker, this session would logically fit after Session 5.

MEMORY VERSE

Do not let any unwholesome talk come out of your mouths, but only what is helpful for building others up according to their needs, that it may benefit those who listen (Eph. 4:29).

KEY PRINCIPLE
Breathe grace rather than judgment.

Suggested Weekly Reading in *The Peacemaker*
- Day 1 – Pages 162–165
- Day 2 – Pages 165–169
- Day 3 – Pages 170–174
- Day 4 – Pages 174–178
- Day 5 – Pages 178–183

THOUGHTS AND QUESTIONS
Thoughts or questions that come to my mind as I read, which I can share with my group:

_____
_____
_____
_____
_____
_____
_____
_____
_____
_____
_____
_____

OPTIONAL SESSION

Part 3—Gently Restore

How can I lovingly serve others by helping them take responsibility for their contribution to this conflict?

Small Group Study

Group Study

Icebreaker

Learning Together (Video)

1. Bring _____ through the gospel (John 4:7–26; 1 Cor. 1:2–9).

2. Be quick to _____.
   Everyone should be quick to listen, slow to speak and slow to become angry (James 1:19; see Prov. 18:13).

3. The tongue of the wise brings _____.
   Reckless words pierce like a sword, but the tongue of the wise brings healing (Prov. 12:18).

   - Breathe grace.
     Do not let any unwholesome talk come out of your mouths, but only what is helpful for building others up according to their needs, that it may benefit those who listen (Eph. 4:29).

   - Speak only to build others up (Eph. 4:29).

   - Make charitable judgments.
     [Love] always protects, always trusts, always hopes, always perseveres (1 Cor. 13:7).

   - Talk in person whenever possible (Matt. 18:15).

- Talk from beside, not from above.
  You hypocrite, first take the plank out of your own eye, and then you will see clearly to remove the speck from your brother's eye (Matt. 7:5).

4. Recognize your _____.
   And the Lord's servant must not quarrel; instead, he must be kind to everyone, able to teach, not resentful. Those who oppose him he must gently instruct, in the hope that God will grant them repentance leading them to a knowledge of the truth, and that they will come to their senses and escape from the trap of the devil, who has taken them captive to do his will (2 Tim. 2:24–26; see Rom. 12:18).

- God's job: To _____ people.

- Your job: To _____ the truth in love.

Key Principle: Breathe grace rather than judgment.

What Do You Think?

1. Watch the "Walls Come Tumbling Down" Peacemaker Parable (a powerful depiction of the effects of an unplanned pregnancy in a pastor's family). Can you relate to anything in this man's behavior? How was he "breathing" judgment to others? How did it affect them? How did he start to breathe grace? How did that affect others?

2. What are some other ways that you or others in your church sometimes aggravate conflict with your tongues? Give examples without identifying specific people.

3. How would viewing yourself as the "chief of sinners" influence the way you speak to others in a conflict?

4. Think of someone who "breathed grace" to you at a stressful time in your life. How did that help you? How would you like to imitate that person as you listen to or speak with others in the future?

5. Describe specific ways that you can bring hope through the gospel. What can you say about who God is, what he is like, and what he is doing that will create an atmosphere in which others will be more willing to confess or hear about their mistakes or wrongs?

6. Describe a situation when you made an uncharitable judgment about someone in your church (i.e., you believed the worst about someone before you had all the facts). What happened? How might your marriage, family, or church change if you and others developed a habit of making charitable judgments?

7. Can you think of a time where you had trouble distinguishing *your job* from *God's job*? What happened? How might it have been different if you had more clearly differentiated between your responsibility and God's responsibility?

Pray for One Another

My Next Step

By God's grace, I will seek to "breathe grace" to several people this week in one of the ways discussed in this session, keeping a journal of how they respond and how it affects these relationships.

Optional Session D
Look Also to the Interests of Others

If keeping in sequence with *The Peacemaker*, this session would logically fit after Session 7.

MEMORY VERSE

Do nothing out of selfish ambition or vain conceit, but in humility consider others better than yourselves. Each of you should look not only to your own interests, but also to the interests of others (Phil. 2:3–4).

KEY PRINCIPLE
When you need to negotiate, PAUSE.

Suggested Weekly Reading in *The Peacemaker*
- Day 1 – Pages 225–228
- Day 2 – Pages 228–231
- Day 3 – Pages 231–233
- Day 4 – Pages 234–240
- Day 5 – Pages 240–245
- Optional – Pages 289–297

THOUGHTS AND QUESTIONS
Thoughts or questions that come to my mind as I read, which I can share with my group:

___
___
___
___
___
___
___
___
___
___

OPTIONAL SESSION

Part 4 – Go and Be Reconciled

How can I demonstrate the forgiveness of God and encourage a reasonable solution to this conflict?

Small Group Study

Group Study

Icebreaker

Learning Together (Video)

1. We negotiate constantly ... but not _____.

2. Competitive negotiation is natural, but _____ (Phil. 2:21).

3. Cooperative negotiation is challenging, but _____.
   Love ... is not self-seeking (1 Cor. 13:4–5; see Matt. 22:39).

   Do nothing out of selfish ambition or vain conceit, but in humility consider others better than yourselves. Each of you should look not only to your own interests, but also to the interests of others (Phil. 2:3–4; see Matt. 7:12 and 1 Cor. 10:24).

4. When you need to negotiate, _____.
   - P_____.
     Those who plan what is good find love and faithfulness (Prov. 14:22).

   - A_____ relationships (Esther 5:1–4).

   - U_____ interests (Phil. 2:1–4; 1 Sam. 25).

   Interests are what really motivate people and give rise to positions. An interest may be a concern, desire, need, limitation, or something a person values or fears.

   [Abigail] fell at his feet and said, "My lord, let the blame be on me alone. Please let your servant speak to you; hear what your servant has to say. . . . [T]he Lord has kept you, my master, from bloodshed and from avenging yourself with your own hands. . . . Let no wrongdoing be found in you as long

as you live. . . . When the Lord has done for my master every good thing he promised concerning him and has appointed him leader over Israel, my master will not have on his conscience the staggering burden of needless bloodshed or of having avenged himself" (1 Sam. 25:24–31).

David said to Abigail, "Praise be to the Lord, the God of Israel, who has sent you today to meet me. May you be blessed for your good judgment and for keeping me from bloodshed this day and from avenging myself with my own hands. Otherwise, as surely as the Lord, the God of Israel, lives, who has kept me from harming you, if you had not come quickly to meet me, not one male belonging to Nabal would have been left alive by daybreak. . . . Go home in peace. I have heard your words and granted your request" (1 Sam. 25:32–35).

- S_____ for creative solutions.

It is the glory of God to conceal a matter; to search out a matter is the glory of kings (Prov. 25:2).

- E_____ options objectively and reasonably.

Daniel then said to the guard whom the chief official had appointed over Daniel, Hananiah, Mishael and Azariah, "Please test your servants for ten days: Give us nothing but vegetables to eat and water to drink. Then compare our appearance with that of the young men who eat the royal food, and treat your servants in accordance with what you see." So he agreed to this and tested them for ten days.

At the end of the ten days they looked healthier and better nourished than any of the young men who ate the royal food. So the guard took away their choice food and the wine they were to drink and gave them vegetables instead (Dan. 1:11–16).

Key Principle: When you need to negotiate, PAUSE.

What Do You Think?

1. Think of a scene in a book or movie in which someone understood and looked out for someone else's interests so effectively that it completely changed the course of the events. Explain how that scene is an example of negotiation?

2. Describe three issues that you negotiate on a regular basis. Do you usually negotiate these types of issues competitively or cooperatively? How do others respond?

3. Think of an issue you need to negotiate with someone. What are some specific ways that you could prepare for your discussion and affirm your respect and appreciation for the other person?

4. Regarding the same issue or a different issue, describe the positions you and the other person are likely to take (e.g., "My husband wants to buy a new car, but I want to redecorate our house.") Try to identify two or three of the interests that might underlie the other person's position—ones you have not considered before. Is there a creative way you might be able to meet some of those interests?

5. How would the unity, productivity, and witness of your church improve if you and other members learned to consistently look "not only to your own interests but also to the interests of others"?

Pray for One Another

My Next Step

I will write a detailed PAUSE plan for an issue I need to negotiate, and then go and put it into practice this week.

Slippery Slope Responses to Conflicts in the Bible

(Answers to the situations described on page 10)

a) Abram combined denial with half-hearted arbitration. Sarai and Hagar verbally assaulted each other, and then Hagar fled (foolish).
b) Joseph fled from Potiphar's wife (wise). She then used assault and litigation by bringing false charges against him (foolish).
c) Joseph's brothers assaulted him (foolish). They eventually confessed their sins, and Joseph forgave and reconciled with them (wise).
d) Saul assaulted and tried to murder David (foolish). David used flight to save his life (wise).
e) Daniel used respectful negotiation (wise).
f) The apostles used mediation or arbitration (it is unclear whether it was merely a suggestion or a binding decision) (wise).
g) Paul used flight to avoid being murdered (wise). Barnabas used mediation to reconcile Paul and the apostles (wise).
h) Paul used accountability (church discipline) to show the seriousness of the immoral Corinthian's sin and possibly bring him to repentance (wise).

God's Response to Conflict
The gospel of Christ is God's perfect response to mankind's sin, rebellion and conflict with him. God overlooks and bears with our sin with great patience (Ps. 103:10–18; Acts 17:30; Rom. 9:22–24), withholding judgment and offering forgiveness and reconciliation in spite of our many offenses against him. The cost for this mercy was immeasurably great; however, God sent his Son to serve as both a mediator (1 Tim. 2:5) and a sacrificial lamb. Jesus went on trial in our place, submitting to civil and religious litigation, was convicted for our sins (2 Cor. 5:21), and suffered the flogging, death, and separation (assault and murder) that we deserve (Mark 15:34). The gospel is the most wonderful and yet costly and painful response to conflict the world has ever seen.

Through the gospel, God has modeled the Four G's of peacemaking perfectly. He revealed the glory of his grace. Although Jesus was without sin, he took our sins as his own, paying for them on the cross. He has shown us our sin and gently restored us. By going from heaven to earth, from earth to the cross, from the cross to the grave, and from the grave to glory, he has secured eternal reconciliation for all who will trust in him.

Answer Key

Session 1
A <u>difference</u> ...
<u>Glorify</u> God
<u>Get</u> the log out ...
<u>Gently</u> restore ...
<u>Go</u> and be ...
<u>Gospel</u> of Christ
<u>Escape</u> responses
<u>Attack</u> responses
<u>Peacemaking</u>

Session 2
Peace with <u>God</u>
Peace with <u>others</u>
Peace within <u>yourself</u>
Jesus' <u>reputation</u>
reconciliation <u>ahead</u>
take the <u>gospel</u>
our <u>lawsuits</u>

Session 3
I <u>desire</u>
I <u>demand</u>
I <u>judge</u>
I <u>punish</u>
asking "<u>X-ray</u>"
<u>Repent</u> and
<u>delight</u> yourself

Session 4
<u>Address</u> everyone
<u>Avoid</u> if
<u>Admit</u> specifically
<u>Acknowledge</u> the
<u>Accept</u> consequences
<u>Alter</u> (change)
<u>Ask</u> for

Session 5
lovingly <u>correct</u>
than <u>confronting</u>
<u>face-to-face</u>
too <u>serious</u>

Session 6
<u>one</u> or <u>two</u>
to the <u>church</u>
a <u>nonbeliever</u>
and <u>restore</u>

Session 7
You <u>cannot</u>
creates a <u>debt</u>
you <u>take</u> payments
Or <u>make</u> payments
is a <u>decision</u>
<u>dwell</u> on
<u>bring</u> up
<u>talk</u> to
<u>stand</u> ... <u>hinder</u>
forgiveness <u>inspires</u>

Session 8
<u>divine</u> weapons
your <u>tongue</u>
godly <u>advisors</u>
what is <u>right</u>
your <u>limits</u>
focused <u>love</u>

OPTIONAL SESSIONS

Optional Session A
a <u>big</u> God
God is <u>sovereign</u>
also <u>all-loving</u>
happens by "<u>chance</u>"
require <u>understanding</u>
been <u>well marked</u>
Trust is a <u>decision</u>

Optional Session B
negative <u>attitude</u>
<u>words</u> or <u>actions</u>
<u>overlook</u> minor
Check your <u>attitude</u>
<u>Rejoice</u> in the Lord
Let your <u>gentleness</u>
<u>Replace</u> anxiety
they <u>really are</u>
<u>Practice</u> what
Count the <u>cost</u>

Optional Session C
Bring <u>hope</u>
quick to <u>listen</u>
brings <u>healing</u>
your <u>limits</u>
<u>change</u> people
<u>speak</u> the truth

Optional Session D
not <u>thoughtfully</u>
but <u>costly</u>
but <u>rewarding</u>
PAUSE
<u>Prepare</u>
<u>Affirm</u>
<u>Understand</u>
<u>Search</u>
<u>Evaluate</u>